Rookie
Read-About® Science

Up and Down

By Patricia J. Murphy

Consultants
Martha Walsh, Reading Specialist

Jan Jenner, Ph.D.

CP Children's Press®
A Division of Scholastic Inc.
New York   Toronto   London   Auckland   Sydney
Mexico City   New Delhi   Hong Kong
Danbury, Connecticut

Designer: Herman Adler Design
Photo Researcher: Caroline Anderson
The photo on the cover shows a group of kids throwing a ball up into the air.

Library of Congress Cataloging-in-Publication Data

Murphy, Patricia J.
    Up and down / by Patricia J. Murphy.
       p. cm. — (Rookie read-about science)
    Includes index.
    Summary: A simple introduction to up and down movement.
    ISBN 0-516-22553-7 (lib. bdg.)   0-516-26866-X (pbk.)
    1. Motion—Juvenile literature. 2. Gravity—Juvenile literature.
[1. Motion. 2. Gravity.] I. Title. II. Series.
QC133.5.M87   2002
531'.113—dc21
                                 2001002688

Up and down. Up and
down. So many things
move up and down.

Light switches move up and down.

Elevators move up and down.

Basketballs move up
and down.

Piano keys move up and down.

How do objects move up
and down?

They start with a force
such as a push or a pull.

You push your arms down
and pull your legs up to
do cartwheels.

You push a window up to open it and pull a window down to close it.

A carpenter pushes a hammer down and pulls the hammer up to pound nails into wood.

Gravity (GRAV-uh-tee) is the pull that holds us down on Earth.

You can see gravity at work when you drop something. The object you drop is pulled down to the ground.

You can feel the pull of gravity when you jump rope. After you push your feet off the ground, you are pulled back down to Earth.

The force of lift can be stronger than gravity.

But when this force gets weak, gravity will pull an object back down.

Wind is a force that
pushes some objects up
into the air.

Wind lifts this kite up
into the air.

When the wind stops, gravity pulls the kite down to the ground.

Up and down. Up and down. So many things move up and down!

Words You Know

carpenter

down

elevator

gravity

pull

push

up

Index

About the Author

Patricia J. Murphy lives in Northbrook, IL, where she writes children's books. She also writes for magazines, corporations, and museums. Most winters, you can find Patricia skiing DOWN (and sometimes falling DOWN) mountains and drinking UP lots of hot cocoa!

Photo Credits

Photographs © 2002: Corbis Stock Market : cover (Norbert Schafer); Corbis-Bettmann: 6 (Duomo), 4 (Owen Franken); Peter Arnold Inc.: 9 (Dimaggio/Kalish), 25, 26, 30 top right, 31 bottom right (James H. Karales); Photo Researchers, NY: 21 (Tim Davis), 3, 29 (Lawrence Migdale); PhotoEdit: 18 (Myrleen Ferguson), 5, 30 bottom left (Spencer Grant), 14, 30 top left (Will Hart); Rigoberto Quinteros: 13, 17, 22, 30 bottom right, 31 bottom left; Visuals Unlimited: 10, 31 top (Tom Edwards), 7 (Gregg Ozzo).